The evil of craving for

WEALTH
and
STATUS

by
Ibn Rajab

D1331652

Translated by
Aboo Talhah Daawood ibn Ronald Burbank

ISBN 1 898649 10 3

British Library Cataloguing in Publication Data.
A catalogue record for this book is available from the British Library.

First Edition, 1415 AH/1995 CE

© Copyright 1995 by Al-Hidaayah Publishing and Distribution

Printed by All Trade Printers, Birmingham, U.K.

Typeset by Al-Hidaayah Publishing & Distribution

Published by   Al-Hidaayah Publishing & Distribution
                  P.O. Box 3332
                  Birmingham
                  United Kingdom
                  B10 9AW

                  Tel: 0121 753 1889
                  Fax: 0121 753 2422

CONTENTS

Publisher's Note

All praise is for Allaah, the Most High. Prayers and peace be upon Muhammad, his family, his Companions and all those who continue in their way until the Day of gathering.

Many a man has led his soul into destruction by that which he covets. Desiring the riches of this world, recognition and authority amongst the people - it was a trial for the nations of the past and many of us relentlessly chase after it today. We hope that this valuable book highlights the evil consequences of craving after wealth and status and how that can corrupt the *Deen* of the Muslim. We pray that this realisation causes our brothers and sisters to race one another in hastening towards forgiveness from Allaah, seeking the best provision in the Hereafter - *aameen*.

This is the English translation of the book *Sharh Hadeeth Maa Dhi'baan Jaa'i'aan...* ("Explanation of the *Hadeeth*: Two Hungry Wolves...") by the esteemed scholar of *Ahlus-Sunnah wal Jamaa'ah*, Imaam al-Haafidh Ibn Rajab al-Hanbalee (d.795H).

May this fine work provide beneficial and thought provoking information for the reader and may it be a treasure for us *On the Day when neither wealth nor sons will benefit (one) except he who comes before Allaah with a sound heart.*

Al-Hidaayah Publishing and Distribution

Note: All references quoted refer to the Arabic books unless otherwise stated.

Editor's Introduction

All praise is for Allaah, we praise Him, we seek His aid and ask for His forgiveness. We seek Allaah's refuge from the evils of ourselves and from our evil actions. Whomsoever Allaah guides then none can misguide him, and whomsoever Allaah misguides then none can guide him. I testify that none has the right to be worshipped except Allaah, alone, having no partner, and I testify that Muhammad is His slave and His Messenger.

To proceed: This is a valuable treatise by al-Haafidh Zaynuddeen 'Abdur-Rahmaan ibn Rajab al-Hanbalee in which he explains the saying of Allaah's Messenger (ﷺ): *"Two hungry wolves let loose among sheep are not more harmful then a person's craving after wealth and status is to his Deen."*

In the treatise he explains the serious consequences of a person's greed for amassing wealth and that it may lead a person into that which is forbidden. Likewise a person's craving after attainment of status and position - then this will generally prevent the good, dignity and honour of the Hereafter - and may lead a person into pride and to looking down upon and having contempt for others.

What is shown by this valuable treatise is applicable to this time of ours and provides a cure for those ailing souls afflicted with love of wealth, who will expend all their efforts in order to amass it - not caring whether they earn it in a way permitted by the *Sharee'ah* or in a way not permitted.

So the Muslim should awaken from this negligence which is caused by the influence of wealth and status and should not miss the opportunity to repent to Allaah and feel remorse for what he has missed - before it is too late.

This treatise was previously printed [in Arabic] within *Ar-Rasaa'il-Muneeriyyah* which was published by Muhammad Muneer ad-Dimashqee in the year 1346H. I present it here afresh, hoping from Allaah, the Most High and the One having full power that it will be pleasing to the noble reader.

I have also added footnotes to the *ahaadeeth* quoted by the author, *rahimahullaah,* quoted their sources and commented upon their level of authenticity as demanded by the principles of the sciences of *hadeeth*. So if I have attained that which is correct - then that is from Allaah, and if I have made any mistake - then that is from me and from Shaitaan.

I hope from Allaah, the Most High, the One having full power that He will accept our righteous actions - indeed He is the Trustee of that and has full power over it.

Badr 'Abdullaah al-Badr
Kuwait
Rabee' uth-Thaanee 1401H.

A Brief Biography of the Author[1]

• He was the *imaam*, the *haafidh*, the great scholar Zaynuddeen 'Abdur-Rahmaan ibn Ahmad ibn 'Abdir-Rahmaan - known as Rajab as-Salaamee, then ad-Dimashqee (from Damascus) - well known as Ibn Rajab.

• He was born in the year 736H.

• His teachers included: Muhammad ibn Khabbaaz, Ibraaheem ibn Daawood al-'Attaar and Muhammad ibn al-Qalaanisee and others.

What the scholars have said about him

• Ibn Fahd said: "The *imaam*, the *haafidh*, the proof, the knowledgeable scholar, the dependable. One of the scholars who shunned this world, and one of the *imaam*s and worshippers. Instructive scholar from the scholars of *hadeeth*, admonisher of the Muslims."

• As-Suyootee said, "The *imaam*, the *haafidh*, the scholar of *hadeeth*, the admonisher, Zaynuddeen 'Abdur-Rahmaan..."

• Ibn Fahd also said, "He was, *rahimahullaahu ta'aala*, a pious *imaam* who shunned the world, hearts inclined towards him with love, and the different sects accepted him. His sittings for advising the general people were of great benefit and used to open up the hearts."

• Ibnul-'Imaad al-Hanbalee said, "al-Haafidh Zaynuddeen, Jamaaluddeen, Abul-Faraj, 'Abdur-Rahmaan - The *shaikh*, the *imaam*, the scholar, the learned, the one who shunned this world, the example..."

---

[1] Taken from the verifiers introduction to the book *Sharh 'Ilalit-Tirmidhee* of the author - with abridgement and editing.

His works

Al-Istikhraaj fee Ahkaamil-Kharaaj (printed), *al-Qawaa'idul-Fiqhiyyah* (printed), *Dhayl Tabaqaatul-Hanaabilah* (printed), *Fadl 'Ilmis-Salaf 'alaa 'Ilmil-Khalaf* (printed), *Lataa'iful-Ma'aarif feemaa limawaasimil-'Aam minal Wazaa'if* (printed), *al-Farq bainan-Naseehah wat-Ta'yeer* (printed), *Sharh Jaami'it-Tirmidhee* (lost except for his explanation of *al-'Ilal* from it), *Sharh Hadeeth Maa Dhi'baan Jaa'i'aan* (this book), and many others.

• He passed away in the year 795H.

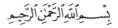

The Evil of Craving for Wealth and Status

All praise is for Allaah, Lord of all the worlds. May Allaah send praises and complete peace until the Day of Recompense upon him, his family and followers and upon all of his Companions.

The Shaikh, the Imaam, the distinguished scholar, Shaikh-ul-Islaam, remainder of the noble *Salaf*, Zaynuddeen Abul-Faraj 'Abdur-Rahmaan, son of the Shaikh and the Imaam Shihaabuddeen Ahmad, son of the Shaikh and the Imaam - Ibn Rajab al-Baghdaadee, al-Hanbalee, *rahimahullaahu ta'aala*, said:

Imaam Ahmad, an-Nasaa'ee, at-Tirmidhee and Ibn Hibbaan in his *Saheeh* report the *hadeeth* of Ka'b ibn Maalik al-Ansaaree, *radiyallaahu 'anhu*, from the Prophet (ﷺ) that he said: *"Two hungry wolves let loose among sheep are not more harmful then a persons craving after wealth and status is to his Deen (Religion)."* at-Tirmidhee said, "It is *hasan saheeh*."[2]

It is also reported from the Prophet (ﷺ) from the *hadeeth* of Ibn 'Umar, Ibn 'Abbaas, Aboo Hurairah, Usaamah ibn Zayd, Jaabir, Aboo Sa'eed al-Khudree and 'Aasim ibn 'Adiyy al-Ansaaree, *radiyallaahu 'anhum 'ajma'een*.[3]

---

[2] It is reported by Ahmad (3/456,460), an-Nasaa'ee in *al-Kubraa* as occurs in *Tuhfatul-Ashraaf* of al-Mizzee (8/316), at-Tirmidhee (no.2376), Ibn Hibbaan (no.2472), Nu'aym ibn Hammaad in his *Zawaa'id* upon *az-Zuhd* (no.181), ad-Daarimee (2/304), at-Tayaalisee (no.2201) and al-Baghawee in *Sharhus-Sunnah* (14/258) and its chain of narration (*isnaad*) is *saheeh* (authentic) as at-Tirmidhee says.

[3] Al-Haithumee quoted most of these narrations in *Majma'uz-Zawaa'id* (10/250) and determined their level of authenticity.

We have mentioned them all and spoken about them in the book *Sharhut-Tirmidhee* (Explanation of *Tirmidhee*).

The wording of the *hadeeth* of Jaabir, *radiyallaahu 'anhu*, is: *"Two ravenous wolves which spend the night amongst sheep whose shepherd is absent, will not cause more havoc for the people than will love of status and wealth to a Believer's Deen."*

In the *hadeeth* of Ibn Abbaas, *radiyallaahu 'anhu*, there occurs, *"love of wealth"* in place of *"craving..."*

This is a very great similitude given to us by the Prophet (ﷺ) to show how the *Deen* of the Muslims is corrupted by craving after wealth and worldly status, and that the damage caused to the *Deen* by it will not be less than the damage caused by two hungry and ravenous wolves which spend the night amongst sheep whose shepherd is absent - so that they feast on them and massacre them.

As is obvious none but a small number of these sheep would escape from the havoc caused by these hungry wolves - and the Prophet (ﷺ) informed us that a person's craving after wealth and status does not cause less harm than these two hungry wolves amongst the sheep. Rather either it will be the same or worse. So this shows that hardly any of a Muslim's *Deen* remains secure if he craves after wealth and status in this world - just as hardly any of the sheep will be saved from the hungry wolves. So this great similitude contains a severe warning against the evil of craving after wealth and status in the world.

Craving for Wealth

The First Type of Craving for Wealth

The first type of craving for wealth is that a person has extreme love for wealth and also relentlessly exerts efforts to attain it - via means which are lawful - being excessive in that, striving hard and making painstaking efforts and toiling in order to attain it.

It has been reported that this *hadeeth* was in response to the appearance of some elements of this, as at-Tabaraanee reports from 'Aasim ibn 'Adiyy, *radiyallaahu 'anhu*, who said, 'I bought a hundred shares from the shares of Khaybar and that reached the Prophet (ﷺ) so he said, *"Two ravenous wolves remaining amongst sheep whose owner has lost them will not be more harmful than a Muslim's seeking after wealth and status is to his Deen."*'[4]

There is nothing more to chasing after wealth than the wastage of a person's noble life for that which has no value. Instead he could have earned a high rank (in Paradise) and everlasting bliss, but he lost this due to his craving after provision - which had already been assured to him and allotted to him, and it was not possible for anything to come to him except what was decreed for him - then on top of this he does not benefit from that, but rather abandons it and leaves it for someone else.

He departs from that and leaves it behind so that he will be the one held accountable for it, yet someone else benefits from it. So in reality he is only gathering it for someone who will not praise him for that, whilst he himself goes on to One who will not excuse him for that - this itself would indeed be enough to show the blameworthiness of this craving.

---

[4] It is quoted by al-Haithumee in *Majma' uz-Zawaa'id* (10/250) and he attributed it to at-Tabaraanee in *al-Awsat* and said, "Its *isnaad* is *hasan* (good)."

The person who has this craving wastes his valuable time and engages himself in that which is of no benefit to himself - in journeying and exposing himself to dangers in order to amass that which will only benefit someone else, so it is as is said:

"So one who spends his days in gathering wealth -
    Out of fear of poverty - then he has achieved only poverty."

It was said to a wise man, "So and so has amassed wealth," so he said, "Then has he amassed days in which to spend it?" It was said, "No." So he said, "Then he has amassed nothing!"

It was also said in some narrations from the People of the Book, "Provision has already been allotted and the one greedy for wealth is deprived. Son of Aadam! If you spend your life in seeking after this world then when will you seek after the Heareafter?" "If you are unable to do good deeds in this world, then what will you do on the Day of Ressurection?"

Ibn Mas'ood, *radiyallaahu 'anhumaa*, said, "Certain faith (*yaqeen*) is that you do not make the people happy by angering Allaah, and that you do not envy anyone for that which Allaah has provided, and that you do not blame anyone for something which Allaah has not given you - since provision will not be brought on by a persons craving after it, nor will it be repelled by a persons disliking it. Indeed Allaah through His Justice has made joy and happiness dependant upon having certain faith and contentment, and He has made worries and sorrow spring from doubt and displeasure."

One of the *Salaf* (predecessors) said: "Since predecree (*qadr*) is a reality then craving is futile. Since treachery exists in people's characters then trusting everybody is to expose oneself to humiliation. Since death awaits everybody, then being satisfied with this world is foolishness."

'Abdul-Waahid ibn Zayd[5] used to swear by Allaah that a person's craving after this world was more fearful to him than his worst enemy. He also used to say, "O my brothers! Do not grow up craving after his riches and increase in earnings or wealth, rather look upon him with the eye of one who detests that he is preoccupying himself with that which will cause his ruin tomorrow in the Place of Return - and is proud with that." He also used to say, "Craving is of two types: Craving which is an affliction and craving which is beneficial. As for the craving which is beneficial, then it is one's desire for that which is obedience to Allaah, and as for the craving which is an affliction - then it is a person's craving after this world."

Craving after this world torments a person, he is preoccupied and does not attain joy or pleasure whilst amassing - since he is preoccupied. He does not find time - due to his love of this world - for the Hereafter, and is preoccupied with that which will perish and forgets that which will abide and remain.

In this regard a person said,
"Do not envy a brother who craves after riches -
        rather look upon him with aversion.
Indeed the one who craves is preoccupied with his
wealth from having any happiness due to his belongings."

Someone else said in this regard:
"O gatherer and miserly one being watched closely by time -
        which is wondering which of its doors it should close.
You have gathered wealth, but think have you gathered for it -
        O gatherer of wealth - days in which you can spend it.
Wealth is hoarded away with you for those who will inherit it -
        The wealth is not yours except on the day when you spend it.

---

[5] From the successors of the *taabi'een* of Basrah, died after 150H.

Satisfaction is for the one who settles in its neighbourhood -
And in its shade he finds no worries to disturb him."

A wise person wrote to a brother of his who desired this world: "To proceed, you have become one who craves after this world. It will serve you whilst taking you away from it with accidents, illnesses, calamities and infirmity. It is as if you have not seen one who craves prevented from what he desires, nor one who shuns this world granted provision, nor one who died despite having great wealth, nor one who is fully satisfied in this world with a small amount."

A desert Arab rebuked a brother of his for covetousness, saying, "O my brother you are a seeker and one sought. You are being sought by One whom you cannot escape, and you are seeking that for which you have been sufficed. O brother, it is as if you have not seen one who craves being prevented, nor one who shuns the world being granted provision."

A wise man said, "The people who have the greatest degree of restlessness are the envious, those who have the greatest degree of happiness are the contented. Those who persevere most through suffering are those who are covetous. Those who have the simplest and most pleasant life are those who most strongly refuse this world. The one who will suffer the greatest regret is the scholar whose actions contradict his knowledge."

The Second Type of Craving After Wealth

The second type of craving after wealth is that in addition to what has been mentioned in the first type, he also seeks wealth through unlawful means and withholds people's rights - then this is definitely blameworthy greed and covetousness. Allaah, the Most High, says:

"And whoever is saved from his covetousness, such are those who are successful."

Soorah al-Hashr (59):9

It is reported in *Sunan Abee Daawood* from 'Abdullaah ibn 'Amr, *radiyallaahu 'anhu*, from the Prophet (ﷺ) that he said, "*Beware of greed (avarice) for indeed greed (avarice) destroyed those who came before you. It ordered them to cut off ties of relationship so they cut off ties of relationship, and it ordered them to be miserly so they were miserly, and it ordered them to commit sins so they committed sins.*"[6]

It is reported in *Saheeh Muslim* from Jaabir, *radiyallaahu 'anhu*, that the Prophet (ﷺ) said, "*Beware of greed (avarice), since greed (avarice) destroyed those who came before you. It led them to shed their blood and make lawful what was forbidden for them.*"[7]

Some of the scholars say, "Avarice is eager craving which causes a person to take things which are not lawful for him, and to withhold

---

[6] Reported by Aboo Daawood (transl. vol.2, p.445, no.1694), and al-Haakim (1/415) who declared it *saheeh* and adh-Dhahabee agreed, and Ahmad reports it (2/159, 195) with similar wording. I say: Its *isnaad* is *saheeh*.

[7] Reported by Muslim (transl. vol.4, p.1366, no. 6248) and others, an-Nawawee said in explanation of the *hadeeth*, "al-Qaadee 'Iyaad said: It is possible that this destruction was the destruction of those whose blood was spilled who were mentioned here, and it is possible that it is destruction in the Hereafter - and this is more apparent, and it is possible that it means destruction in both this world and the Hereafter. A number of people have said that avarice/greed (*shuhh*) is more severe than miserliness (*bukhl*) and causes the person to withhold to a greater degree. Some say that it is miserliness combined with covetousness. Some say that miserliness is with reference to specific actions whereas avarice/greed is general. Some say that miserliness is in particular actions and avarice/greed is with reference to wealth and good actions. Others say that avarice/greed is desiring that which one does not possess and being miserly about what one does possess."

the rights of others. Its reality is that a person craves that which Allaah has forbidden and prohibited him from, and that one is not contented with the wealth and womenfolk and whatever else Allaah has made lawful for him. So Allaah, the Most High, has made lawful for us that which is good from foods, drinks, clothing and women and has forbidden us to acquire these things except by lawful means and He made lawful for us the blood and wealth of the Unbelievers and those fighting against us. He also forbade us from everything impure from foods, drinks, clothing and women, and He forbade us from seizing people's wealth and spilling their blood unjustly. So he who limits himself to that which is permitted for him is a Believer, and one who goes beyond that into what he has been forbidden - then this is blameworthy avarice which is inconsistent with *Eemaan* (true faith in belief, word and action).

Therefore the Prophet (ﷺ) informed that avarice causes a person to cut off relations, commit sins and to be miserly - and miserliness is a person's clinging on greedily to what he has in his hand. Whereas avarice is seeking to obtain that which does not belong to him unjustly and wrongfully - whether it is wealth or something else. It is even said that it is the head of all sins - this was how Ibn Mas'ood, *radiyallaahu 'anhu*, and others from the *Salaf* explained avarice and greed.

So from this the meaning of the *hadeeth* of Aboo Hurairah, *radiyallaahu 'anhu*, will be understood. He reports that the Prophet (ﷺ) said, "*Avarice (shuhh) and Eemaan will not combine in the heart of a Believer.*"[8] Also in another *hadeeth* from the Prophet (ﷺ) he

---

[8] This is part of a *hadeeth* whose wording is, "*Dust in the way of Allaah and the smoke of Hell-Fire will never combine in the belly of a servant, nor will avarice and Eemaan ever combine in the heart of a servant.*" It is reported by Ibn Abee Shaibah (5/344), Ahmad, an-Nasaa'ee (6/13,14)... and its chain of narration is *hasan lighairihi* (good due to supports).

said, *"The best of Eemaan is self-restraint (sabr) and compliance/ liberality (musaamahah),"*[9] *Sabr* here has been explained to be withholding oneself from forbidden things, and *musaamahah* as the carrying out of the obligatory actions.

Also the word *shuhh* (avarice) may sometimes be used to mean *bukhl* (miserliness) and vice-versa, however in origin they are different in meaning as we have mentioned.

If the person's craving after wealth reaches this level then the deficiency it causes in a person's Religion is clear - since failing to fulfil what is obligatory and falling into what is forbidden reduce one's Religion and *Eemaan* without a doubt to the point that nothing but a little remains of it.

---

[9] This *hadeeth* has been reported from four Companions: (i) 'Umayr ibn Qataadah al-Laythee, by al-Bukhaaree in *at-Taareekhul-Kabeer* (3/2/530) and al-Haakim (3/626), (ii) Jaabir ibn 'Abdillaah - by Ibn Abee Shaibah in *al-Eemaan* (no.43) and Ibn Hibbaan in *al-Majrooheen* (3/136), (iii) 'Amr ibn 'Abasah - by Ahmad (4/375) and (iv) 'Ubaadah ibn as-Saamit - by Ahmad (5/319), and the *hadeeth* is *saheeh* due to these chains - and Allaah knows best.

Craving for Status

A person's craving after status is even more destructive than his craving after wealth. Seeking after worldly status, position, leadership and domination causes more harm to a person than his seeking after wealth - it is more damaging and harder to avoid since even wealth is expended in seeking after leadership and status. Craving after status is of two types:

The First Type of Craving for Status

The first is seeking status through authority, leadership, and wealth and this is very dangerous - since it will usually prevent a person from the good of the Hereafter and nobility and honour in the next life, Allaah, the Most High, says:

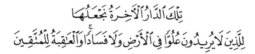

"That home of the Hereafter We shall assign to those who seek neither haughtiness nor any corruption on earth. The good end is for the pious."

al-Qasas (28): 83

So it is rare that a person seeks after position in this world by seeking authority and is guided to and granted what is good for him. Rather he is entrusted to his own self, just as the Prophet (ﷺ) said to 'Abdur-Rahmaan ibn Samurah, *radiyallaahu 'anhu, "O 'Abdur-Rahmaan! Do not ask for authority since if you are given it due to requesting it then you are abandoned to it, but if you are given it without requesting it then you will be aided in it."*[10]

---

[10] Reported by Ahmad and al-Bukhaaree (transl. 9/194/no.260).

One of the *Salaf* said, "No one seeks after authority and then behaves justly in it." Yazeed ibn 'Abdillaah ibn Mawhib was a just judge and one of the righteous people and he used to say, "Whoever loves wealth and status and fears adversity will not behave with justice." There occurs in *Saheeh al-Bukhaaree* from Aboo Hurairah, *radiyallaahu 'anhu*, from the Prophet (ﷺ) that he said, *"You will be keen to attain authority and it will be a source of regret on the Day of Resurrection. So what an excellent wet-nurse it is and what an evil weaner."*[11]

(Al-Bukhaaree) also reports from Aboo Moosa al-Ash'aree, *radiyallaahu 'anhu*, that two men said to the Prophet (ﷺ), 'O Messenger of Allaah! Appoint us to some position of authority.' So he said, *"We do not appoint to authority in this affair of ours one who requests it, nor one who is keen to have it."*[12]

---

[11] Reported by al-Bukhaaree (transl. 9/196/no.262) and others. Note: His saying, *"It will be a source of regret,"* means one who does not behave correctly having attained it - and the proof for this is what Muslim reports from Aboo Dharr who said, *'I said, "O Messenger of Allaah! Will you not appoint me to some position?" He said, "You are weak and it is a trust and on the Day of Resurrection it will be a source of humiliation and regret, except for one who fulfils its obligations and carries out the duties required from him."* (*Saheeh Muslim*, transl.3/1015/4491). An-Nawawee said, "This is a great reason to avoid positions of authority especially those who are weak - and this refers to those who are not suitable and those who do not act justly in the position - then he will regret his negligence when he is humiliated on the Day of Resurrection. However one who is suitable for the position and behaves justly in it - then there is a great reward as shown in a number of reports. However entering into it carries a great danger therefore the great scholars avoided it. His saying, *"What a good wet-nurse"* (i.e. the one who feeds the baby at the breast) meaning in this world, and *"What an evil weaner"* meaning after death - since he will be taken to account for it. So he is like one who is weaned away from breast milk before he can manage without it - so this causes his destruction. And it is said, *"What a good wet nurse"* due to the status, wealth, authority, attainment of physical and imagined enjoyment which it produces whilst one has it, but *"What an evil weaner"* meaning when one is removed from it by death or other causes - due to the evil consequences one faces in the Hereafter." (Abridged and edited from *Fathul-Baaree* of Ibn Hajar (13/125-126)).

[12] Reported by al-Bukhaaree (transl. 9/196/no.263) and Muslim (transl. 3/1014/no.4489)

Know that craving after status and position inevitably causes great harm before its attainment due to the striving necessary to attain it, and also afterwards due to the person's strong desire to hold onto it which produces injustice, haughtiness and other evils.

Aboo Bakr al-Aajurree, who was one of the wise scholars and teachers at the start of the fourth century, wrote a treatise about the manners and the sentiments of the scholars and it is one of the best works on this topic. One who studies it will know from it the way of the scholars of the *Salaf*, and will know the innovated ways contrary to their way. So he describes the evil scholar at length, from this description is that: 'He has become infatuated with love of this world, and with praise, honour and position with the people of this world. He uses knowledge as an adornment just as a beautiful woman adorns herself with jewellery for this world, but he does not adorn his knowledge with action upon it." He then mentions a lengthy speech and then says, "So these characteristics and their like predominate in the heart of one who does not benefit from knowledge, so whilst he carries these attributes his soul will come to have love of status and position - so that he loves to sit with kings and the sons of this world. Then he loves to share in their opulent lifestyle, sharing their lavish attire, their comfortable transport, servants, fine clothing, delicate bedding and delicious food. He will love that people throng to his door, that his saying is listened to, and that he is obeyed - and he can only attain the latter by becoming a judge (*qaadee*) - so he seeks to become one. Then he is unable to attain it except at the expense of his Religion, so he debases himself to the rulers and their helpers, serving them himself and giving them his wealth as a tribute. He remains silent when he sees their evil actions after entering their palaces and homes. Then on top of this he may praise their evil actions and declare them good due to some false interpretation in order to raise his position with them. So when he has accustomed himself to doing this over a long period of time and falsehood has taken root in him - then they appoint him to the position of judge (*qaadee*) and in so doing slaughter him without a knife."[13]

Then they have bestowed such a favour upon him that he is obliged and has to show his gratitude to them - so he takes great pains to make sure that he does not anger them and cause them to remove him from his position. But he has no concern about whether he angers his Lord, the Most High, so he misappropriates the wealth of orphans, widows, the poor and the needy, and wealth bequested as *waqf* (religious endowment) for those fighting *Jihaad* and the nobles of Makkah and al-Madeenah, and wealth which is supposed to be of benefit to all the Muslims - but instead he uses it to satisfy his clerk, chamberlain and servant. So he eats that which is *haraam* and feeds with that which is *haraam* and increases that which is a proof against him. So woe to the one whose knowledge causes him to have these characteristics. Indeed this is the knowledge which the Prophet (ﷺ) sought refuge from and ordered us to seek refuge from. This is the knowledge which the Prophet (   ) mentioned, saying, *"Those amongst the people receiving the severest punishment on the Day of Resurrection is the scholar who is not given benefit through his knowledge by Allaah."*[14] He (ﷺ) used to say,

اللَّهُمَّ ! إِنِّي أَعُوذُ بِكَ مِنَ الأَرْبَعِ : مِنْ عِلْمٍ لا يَنْفَعُ ، وَمِنْ قَلْبٍ لا يَخْشَعُ ، وَمِنْ نَفْسٍ لا تَشْبَعُ ، وَمِنْ دُعَاءٍ لا يُسْمَعُ

---

[13] Alluding to the saying of the Prophet (ﷺ), *"He who is appointed as a judge has been killed without a knife."* Reported by Ahmad, Aboo Daawood (transl. 3/1013/ no.3564) and at-Tirmidhee who declared it *hasan*. I say: Its *isnaad* is *saheeh*.

[14] Reported by Ibn 'Abdul-Barr in *Jaami' Bayaanil-'Ilm* (1/162) and al-Aajurree (pp.93-94) and at-Tabaraanee in *as-Sagheer* (1/1831) and others and its chain of narration is very weak since it contains 'Uthmaan ibn Miqsam al-Burree who was accused of lying and fabrication. It is however reported as being the saying of Abud-Dardaa only, with an authentic chain of narration. It is reported by ad-Daarimee (1/ 82) and others.

(Allaahumma innee a'oodhubika minal arba'i, min 'ilmin laa yanfa'u, wa min qalbin laa yakhsha'u, wa min nafsin laa tashba'u, wa min du'aa in laa yusma'u)

"O Allaah I seek Your refuge from knowledge which does not benefit; from a heart which does not fear; from a soul which is never satisfied; and from a supplication which is not heard."[15]

And he (ﷺ) used to say,

اللَّهُمَّ إِنِّي أَسْأَلُكَ عِلْماً نَافِعاً ، وَأَعُوذُ بِكَ مِنْ عِلْمٍ لَا يَنْفَعُ

(Allaahumma innee as'aluka 'ilman naafi'an, wa a'oodhubika min 'ilmin laa yanfa'u)

"O Allaah I ask You for beneficial knowledge, and I seek Your refuge from knowledge which does not benefit."[16]

This was said by Imaam Aboo Bakr al-Aajurree, *rahimahullaahu ta'aala*, who lived at the end of the fourth century[17] and corruption increased and multiplied greatly since his time - and there is no might and no strength except by Allaah's will.

---

[15] Reported by Ahmad, Aboo Daawood (transl. vol.1/p.401/no.1543) and others, all with the wording, *"O Allaah I seek Your refuge from four: from knowledge which does not benefit..."* The *hadeeth* was declared to be *saheeh* by al-Haakim and adh-Dhahabee agreed, and it has supports from a number of the Companions.

[16] Reported with this wording by al-Aajurree (p.134) and Ibn Hibbaan (no.2426). It is also reported by Ibn Maajah (no.3843) and Ibn 'Abdul-Barr (1/162) with the wording, *"Ask Allaah for beneficial knowledge and seek Allaah's refuge from knowledge which does not benefit."* Its chain of narration is *hasan* (good) and there is a similar narration from Umm Salamah reported by Ibn Maajah and others.

[17] Al-Aajurree, *rahimahullaah*, died in the year 360H.

From the subtle afflictions caused by love of status is seeking after and aspiring positions of authority - this is something whose reality is hidden and obscure. It is not understood except by those who have knowledge of Allaah, those who love Him and who are at enmity with those ignorant one's from His creation who desire to compete with Him with regard to His Lordship and Divinity and right to worship, despite their despicability and the contemptible position they have before Allaah and in the eyes of His chosen servants who have knowledge of Him. It is just as al-Hasan (al-Basree), *rahimahullaah*, said about them, "Even if the hooves of mules clatter for them and riding beasts strut for them, yet still the humiliation of sin rests upon their necks. Allaah has refused except that He will humiliate those who are disobedient to Him." Know that love of status attained by having one's orders and prohibitions obeyed and enacted, and by being in charge of the people's affairs - if what is intended by this is merely the attainment of a position above the people and to have importance over them, and that it be seen that the people are in need of him and seek their needs from him - then the soul of this person is seeking to compete with Allaah in His Lordship and His Divinity and right to worship. Some such people may even seek to put the people into such a condition of need that they are compelled to request their needs from them, and to display their poverty before them and their need of them. Then he is inflated with pride and self-importance because of that, whereas this befits none except Allaah alone, He who has no partner. Allaah, the Most High, says,

وَلَقَدْ أَرْسَلْنَآ إِلَىٰٓ أُمَمٍ مِّن قَبْلِكَ فَأَخَذْنَٰهُم بِٱلْبَأْسَآءِ وَٱلضَّرَّآءِ لَعَلَّهُمْ يَتَضَرَّعُونَ

"Verily, We sent (Messengers) to many nations before you (O Muhammad (ﷺ)). And We seized them with extreme poverty (or loss in wealth) and loss in health with calamities so that they might believe with humility."

al-An'aam (6):42

23

$$وَمَآ أَرْسَلْنَا فِى قَرْيَةٍ مِّن نَّبِىٍّ إِلَّآ$$

$$أَخَذْنَآ أَهْلَهَا بِٱلْبَأْسَآءِ وَٱلضَّرَّآءِ لَعَلَّهُمْ يَضَّرَّعُونَ ٩٤$$

"And We sent no Prophet unto any town (and they denied him), but We seized its people with suffering from extreme poverty (or loss in wealth) and loss of health and calamities, so that they may humiliate themselves (and repent to Allaah)."

al-A'raaf (7): 94

It also occurs in some narrations that Allaah, the Most High, sends adversity upon His servant in order to hear him call upon him with full humility. There also occurs in the narrations that when the servant whom Allaah loves supplicates to Allaah, the Most High, then He, the Most High, says, "O Jibreel! Do not hasten to carry out his need, for I love that I should hear him calling with full humility."[18] So these matters are worse and more dangerous than mere injustice and are more sinister, and they are a part of *shirk* - and *shirk* is the greatest injustice and transgression with Allaah. It is reported in the *Saheeh* from the Prophet (ﷺ) that he said, *"Allaah, the Most High, says, 'Pride is my cloak and majesty is my lower-garment so whoever vies with Me regarding them I will punish him.'"*[19]

---

[18] The meaning of this is reported in a *hadeeth qudsee* which is mentioned by Shaikh Muhammad al-Madanee in his book *al-Ittihaafaatus-Sunniyyah fil-Ahaadeethil-Qudsiyyah* (no.438) - and he mentioned that Ibn 'Asaakir reported it with a chain of narration containing Ishaaq ibn 'Abdillaah ibn Abee Farwah who is abandoned as a narrator.

[19] Reported by Ahmad, Aboo Daawood (transl. 3/1141/no.4079) and Ibn Maajah from the *hadeeth* of Ibn Maajah, except that their wording ends, "...So whoever vies with Me regarding any one of them..." and in a wording, *"...anything from them, I will fling him into Hell-Fire."* and in a wording, *"...the Fire."* Its chain of narration is *saheeh*. Muslim (transl. 4/1381/no.6349) also reports one version of the *hadeeth*.

It also happened that one of the people of the past was a judge and he saw in a dream that someone was saying to him, "You are a judge and Allaah is a Judge." So he awoke in a distressed state and removed himself from the position of judge and abandoned it.

Some of the pious judges used to prevent the people from calling them 'Judge of judges' (Qaadiyyul-Qudaat) since this name resembles the name 'King of kings' which the Prophet (ﷺ) censured that one should use as a title, and 'Judge of judges' is like it.

Also related to this is that the one having status and authority loves that he is praised and commended for his actions and seeks that from the people. Those who do not comply with this suffer as a result. It may even be that his actions are actually more deserving of blame than of praise, or he manifests something that is apparently good - and loves to be praised for it, yet in reality he is intending something evil and is happy that he is able to deceive the people and fool them about it. This falls under the saying of Allaah, the Most High:

$$لَا تَحْسَبَنَّ ٱلَّذِينَ يَفْرَحُونَ بِمَآ أَتَوا۟ وَّيُحِبُّونَ أَن يُحْمَدُوا۟ بِمَا لَمْ يَفْعَلُوا۟ فَلَا تَحْسَبَنَّهُم بِمَفَازَةٍ مِّنَ ٱلْعَذَابِ وَلَهُمْ عَذَابٌ أَلِيمٌ ۝١٨٨$$

"Think not that those who rejoice in what they have done (or brought about), and love to be praised for what they have not done, think not that they are rescued from the torment, and for them is a painful torment."

Aal-'Imraan (3):188

Since this *Aayah* was sent down regarding those who have these attributes, and this attribute (i.e. seeking praise from the creation and loving it and punishing those who do not give it) is not fitting except for Allaah, alone, having no partner. This is why the rightly guided leaders used to forbid people to praise them for their actions and any good which they did, and they would order that rather praise be given to Allaah alone, having no partner - since all blessings are from Him.

'Umar ibn 'Abdul-'Azeez, *rahimahullaah*, was very particular about this and he once wrote a letter to be read out to the people performing Hajj. It contained an order that they should be treated well and that oppression of them should stop, and in it there occurred, "And do not praise anyone for this except Allaah, since if He abandoned me to my own devices I would be just like the others."

There is also a well-known narration about what occurred with him concerning the woman who requested from him that he should provide an allowance for her orphaned daughters. She had four daughters and he gave an allowance to two of them and she praised Allaah. Then he gave an allowance to the third so she thanked him, so he said, "We were giving an allowance to them as long as you were giving praise to the One to whom it is due, but now order this third one to share her allowance with the fourth," or as he said, *radiyallaahu 'anhu*. He wanted to make it known that the position of leadership is only established so that Allaah's commands are carried out, and so that the servants can be commanded to obey Allaah, the Most High, and forbidden from those things which Allaah has prohibited, and so that the leader acts with sincerity towards Allaah's servants by calling them to Allaah. His intention is that the *Deen* should in its entirety be for Allaah, and that honour be for Allaah. Along with this he is fearful that he is himself falling short with regard to the rights of Allaah, the Most High.

So as for those who love Allaah, then the limit of their desire with regard to the creation is that they should also love Allaah, obey Him and single Him out with all worship and recognise His Divinity alone. (Then how about one who seeks to vie with Him in this?!) Rather this type of person does not desire any reward or any thanks from the creation, but hopes for reward for his actions from Allaah, the Most High:

مَاكَانَ لِبَشَرٍ أَن يُؤْتِيَهُ اللَّهُ الْكِتَـٰبَ
وَالْحُكْمَ وَالنُّبُوَّةَ ثُمَّ يَقُولَ لِلنَّاسِ كُونُوا عِبَادًا لِّي مِن
دُونِ اللَّهِ وَلَـٰكِن كُونُوا رَبَّـٰنِيِّنَ بِمَا كُنتُمْ تُعَلِّمُونَ الْكِتَـٰبَ
وَبِمَا كُنتُمْ تَدْرُسُونَ ۝ وَلَا يَأْمُرَكُمْ أَن تَتَّخِذُوا الْمَلَـٰئِكَةَ
وَالنَّبِيِّـۧنَ أَرْبَابًا أَيَأْمُرُكُم بِالْكُفْرِ بَعْدَ إِذْ أَنتُم مُّسْلِمُونَ ۝

"It is not (possible) for any human being to whom Allaah has given *al-Hukma* (knowledge and understanding of the laws of Religion etc.) and Prophethood to say to the people: "Be my worshippers rather than Allaah's.' On the contrary (he would say): 'Be you *rabbaaniyyoon* (learned men of Religion, who practice what they know and also preach to others) because you teach the Book, and you study it.' Nor would he order you to take angels and Prophets for lords (gods). Would he order you to disbelieve after you have submitted to Allaah's Will?"

Aal-'Imraan (3):79-80

He (ﷺ) said, *"Do not exaggerate in praising me as the Christians praised the Messiah, the son of Maryam. Indeed I am only a slave. So say the slave of Allaah and His Messenger."*[20] Allaah's Messenger (ﷺ) also used to criticise anyone who did not keep to this manner of address with regard to him, just as he (ﷺ) said, *"Do not say,*

---

[20] Reported by al-Bukhaaree (transl.vol.4, p.435, no.654) and others.

'Whatever Allaah has willed and Muhammad has willed,' but rather say, 'Whatever Allaah has willed, then what Muhammad has willed.'"[21]

He also replied to a person who said, "Whatever Allaah and yourself have willed," by saying, *"Have you made me a rival for Allaah! Rather say, 'Whatever Allaah alone has willed.'*"[22]

Due to this the *khulafaa'* who succeeded the Prophets, and their followers - the just rulers and their successors, and their judges never used to call to glorification of themselves but rather to the glorification of Allaah alone and that He is to be singled out with worship and divinity. From them were those who did not wish for leadership at all except as an aid to calling to Allaah alone. Some of the righteous people who accepted the position of judge said, "Indeed I accepted this in order to use it to help me in ordering the good and forbidding the evil."

Indeed the Messengers and their followers would persevere in the face of injury and harm which they suffered whilst calling to Allaah, and in carrying out Allaah's commands they were put into the severest hardship by the people and yet they bore it with patience. Indeed being pleased with that, since one who has love may find pleasure in any harm he meets whilst seeking to please the one whom he loves. Just as 'Abdul-Maalik ibn 'Umar ibn 'Abdul-Azeez used to say to his father when he was the *khaleefah* and he had keen desire that the

---

[21] Reported by ad-Daarimee (2/295) with this wording and its chain of narration is *saheeh*. It is also reported with the wording, *"Do not say, 'Whatever Allaah and so and so have willed,' but rather say, 'Whatever Allaah has willed and then what so and so has willed.'"* It is reported by Ahmad, Aboo Daawood (transl. vol.3, p.1386, no.4962) and others and its chain of narration is *saheeh*.

[22] Reported by Ahmad, al-Bukhaaree in *al-Aadaabul-Mufrad* (no.783) and others, and its chain of narration is *hasan*.

truth and justice be established, "O father I would have loved that we had been forced into boiling cooking pots for the sake of Allaah, the Mighty and Majestic."

Another righteous person said, "I would have loved that my flesh were cut away with scissors if it meant that all the creation would obey Allaah, the Mighty and Majestic." This saying of his was related to a certain wise person, so he said, "If what he was speaking of was sincere concern for the creation, otherwise I do not know." Then he fainted. The meaning of this is that the one who said this had true and sincere concern for the creation and pity for them, fearing Allaah's punishment for them, so he would have loved that they could have been saved from Allaah's punishment at the expense of his own self. It could also be that he was considering the Majesty and Greatness of Allaah and the glorification, honour, obedience and love due to Him, so he wished that the creation would fulfil that even if it meant the most severe harm to himself. This is the state of mind of the distinguished ones who love Allaah and have knowledge of Him and keep Him in mind. This is what caused the man to faint.

Allaah, the Most High, also described in His Book those who love Him as being those who fight *Jihaad* in His cause and do not fear the blame of those who seek to blame.[23]
Concerning this someone said:
"I find that being blamed whilst pursuing what you desire is delightful,
> For having love for your remembrance let those who wish to blame me do so."

---

[23] Sooratul-Maa'idah (5):54

The Second Type of Craving for Status

The second type of eeking status and position over the people is through matters of the *Deen* such as knowledge, action and *zuhd* (shunning this world and its delights). This is more wicked that the first type, more disgraceful, more corrupt and more dangerous. This is because knowledge, action and shunning of this world are for seeking the high ranks and never-ending bliss that are with Allaah, and to seek nearness to Allaah.

Ath-Thawree,[24] "The excellence of knowledge is due only to the fact that it causes a person to fear and obey Allaah, otherwise it is just like anything else." So if a person seeks through any of this some worldly end, then this is also of two types:

The first type is he who seeks wealth through it - then this is a part of craving after wealth and seeking it through forbidden means. Concerning this there is the *hadeeth* from the Prophet (ﷺ), *"Whoever seeks knowledge from that by which Allaah's Face is sought but does not learn it except for some worldly goal, then he will not smell the fragrance of Paradise on the Day of Resurrection."* It is reported by Imaam Ahmad, Aboo Daawood, Ibn Maajah and Ibn Hibbaan in his *Saheeh* from the *hadeeth* of Aboo Hurairah from the Prophet (ﷺ).[25]

The reason for this, and Allaah knows best, is that in this world there is a foretaste of Paradise and it is knowledge of Allaah, love of Him, being happy with Him, longing to meet Him, fearing Him and obeying Him. The way to this is shown by beneficial knowledge and he

---

[24] Sufyaan ibn Sa'eed ath-Thawree, famous *imaam* from the successors of the *taabi'een*. Ibnul-Mubaarak said, "I have not written from anyone more excellent than him." He died at the age of 64 in Sha'baan 161H.

[25] Aboo Daawood (transl.vol.3, p.1039, no.3656) and others. Its chain of narration contains Fulaih ibn Sulaimaan who is acceptable but has a poor memory - however another narrator supports his narration in the report of Ibn 'Abdul-Barr in *al-Jaami'* (1/190) so the *hadeeth* is *saheeh*.

whose knowledge leads him to experience this foretaste of Paradise in this world will enter Paradise in the Hereafter, and he who does not smell its fragrance will not smell the fragrance of Paradise in the Hereafter.

Therefore the one who receives the severest punishment in the Hereafter is the scholar to whom Allaah does not grant the benefit of his knowledge. He is one of those people who will suffer the most severe regret on the Day of Resurrection since he had what was required to take him to the highest levels and most elevated stations [in Paradise] yet he used it only to attain the most lowly, inferior and contemptible ends. So he is like a man who had valuable and expensive pearls and sold them for a piece of animal dung, or something filthy and of no use. This is the condition of one who seeks this world with his knowledge, rather he is worse. Worse still is one who seeks it by outwardly displaying that he is one who abstains from this world - this is a very despicable deception.

Sulaymaan ad-Daaraanee used to criticise a person who wore a simple coarse cloak if he had some worldly desire in his heart greater than the value of the cloak. What he was indicating was that manifesting one's aversion to this world by wearing clothes showing connection to the Religion only befits one whose heart is empty of any attachment to it - such that his heart has no greater attachment to it than the value of the clothes he is seen to be wearing, so that he is the same outwardly and inwardly with regard to his disassociation from this world.

How well a certain wise person spoke when asked about the (true) *Soofee*,[26] so he replied,

---

[26] What the author means by *Soofee*, is one who abstains from the world and engages in much worship and not the modern day usage of the term referring to the group of people who are immersed in innovation both in their beliefs and actions - may Allaah protect us. [Publisher's Note]

"He who wears the woollen clothes on top of purity and sincerity, whilst following the way of the Chosen Messenger:
    Who tastes delight despite experiencing harshness,
And the world is thrown behind his neck."

The second type is he who through his knowledge, action and shunning of this world seeks: leadership of the people and a position of honour above them and that the creation should comply and submit to him and turn their faces to him. He seeks that it should become manifest to the people that he has greater knowledge than the scholars so that he can attain a status greater than theirs and so on. The appointed place for a person like this is the Hell-Fire. This is because intending to arrogantly raise oneself above the creation is itself something forbidden, then if one seeks it through the means of attaining the Hereafter then this is worse and more despicable than attempting it through use of worldly means such as wealth and leadership.

There occurs in the *Sunan* a narration from the Prophet (ﷺ), *"Whoever seeks knowledge in order to argue with the ignorant and to argue with the scholars, or to turn the people's faces towards him, then Allaah will enter him into the Fire."* It is reported by Imaam Ahmad and at-Tirmidhee from the *hadeeth* of Ka'b ibn Maalik.[27] Ibn Maajah reports it from the *hadeeth* of Ibn 'Umar, *radiyallaahu 'anhumaa,* and Hudhayfah, *radiyallaahu 'anhu,* and his wording is, *"..then he is*

---

[27] Reported by at-Tirmidhee (no.2654), al-Haakim (1/86) and al-Aajurree(p.93). At-Tirmidhee said, "This is a singular (*ghareeb*) *hadeeth*, we do not know it except from this narration, and Ishaaq ibn Yahyaa ibn Talhah [one of its narrators] is not very strong in their view, some of them speak about him concerning his memory." I say: Ibn Hajr says of him in *at-Taqreeb*, "Weak." However it is strengthened by the following narration.

in the fire."[28]

Ibn Maajah and Ibn Hibbaan in his *Saheeh* report the *hadeeth* of Jaabir, *radiyallaahu 'anhu*, from the Prophet (ﷺ) who said, *"Do not seek knowledge in order to compete with the scholars, nor to argue with the ignorant, nor to gain ascendancy in the assemblies. So whoever does that, then the Fire, the Fire!"*[29]

Ibn Adiyy reports its like from the *hadeeth* of Aboo Hurairah, *radiyallaahu 'anhu*, from the Prophet (ﷺ), and he added, *"...Rather learn it for the Face of Allaah and the Hereafter."*[30] Also from Ibn Mas'ood, *radiyallaahu 'anhumaa*, who said, "Do not learn knowledge for three: To argue with it with the ignorant, nor to contend with the scholars through it, nor to turn the people's faces towards yourselves. Rather seek by your saying and action that which is with Allaah - since it will remain and everything else will perish."[31]

---

[28] The *hadeeth* of Ibn 'Umar has two chains from him, the first is reported by Ibn Maajah (no.258), at-Tirmidhee (no.2655) who declared it *hasan* and al-Aajurree (p.92), and its chain of narration is *munqati'* (disconnected). The second is reported by Ibn Maajah (no.253) and its chain of narration contains a weak narrator and one who is unknown. As for the *hadeeth* of Hudhayfah, then it has three chains, the first is reported by Ibn Maajah (no.259) and its chain of narration contains Ash'ath ibn Sawwaar who is weak. The second is reported by al-Khateeb in *Iqtidaa ul-'Ilmil-'Amal* (no.100) and contains Basheer ibn 'Ubayd al-Madaarisee who is weak and is accused of lying. The third is reported by al-Khateeb in his *Taareekh* (9/446-447) and contains Aboo Bakr ad-Daahiree who is abandoned and accused of lying.

[29] Reported by Ibn Maajah (no.253), Ibn Hibbaan (no.90: *Mawaarid*) and others. Its chain of narration here is weak since it contains Ibn Juraij and Abuz-Zubayr, both of whom are *mudallis* reporting with *'an'anah* [not clearly stating that he heard it directly from the narrator before him]. However the *hadeeth* is established since the author will mention a *hasan* (good) chain of narration for it afterwards.

[30] Al-Khateeb reports it in *al-Faqeeh wal-Mutafaqqih* (2/88) from Ibn 'Adiyy with it and its chain of narration is *hasan*.

[31] It is reported by al-Khateeb in *al-Faqeeh wal-Mutafaqqih* (2/88-89) and its chain of narration is weak since it contains Muhammad ibn 'Awn al-Khuraasaanee who is abandoned (*matrook*).

It is also established in *Saheeh Muslim* from Aboo Hurairah, *radiyallaahu 'anhu*, from the Prophet (ﷺ) who said, *"The first of the creation for whom the Fire will be kindled on the Day of Resurrection are three... from them is the scholar who recited the Qur'aan in order for it to be said that he is a reciter, and he learned knowledge in order for it to be said that he is a scholar, and it will be said to him, "That was said," then the order will be given regarding him and he will be dragged upon his face and flung into the Fire."* He mentioned the same regarding the one who gives charity in order for it to be said that he is generous, and the one who fights *Jihaad* in order for it to be said that he is a brave person.[32]

Also from 'Alee, *radiyallaahu 'anhu*, who said, "O bearers of knowledge! Act upon it since the scholar is the one who acts upon what he knows, so that his actions conform to his knowledge. For there will come a people who carry knowledge but it does not penetrate beyond their throats. Their knowledge will be contrary to their actions, and what they hide will be contrary to what they manifest. They will sit in circles and vie with one another to the point that a man will become angry with one who sits with him if he sits with someone else and abandons him. Their actions in those assemblies of theirs will not be raised up to Allaah, the Mighty and Majestic."

Al-Hasan [al-Basree] said, "Do not let the share of knowledge that one of you possesses be merely that the people say that he is a scholar." It also occurs in some reports that 'Eesaa, *'alaihis-salaam*, said, "How can a person be from the people of knowledge if he only seeks knowl-

---

[32] The *hadeeth* is reported by Ahmad (2/322), Muslim (transl. vol.3, p.1055, no.4688), an-Nasaa'ee (6/23-24) and others, however the *hadeeth* which they report begins, *"The first of the people against whom judgement will be passed..."* As for the wording, *"The first of the creation for whom the Fire will be kindled on the Day of Resurrection."* then it is reported by Ibnul-Mubaarak in *az-Zuhd* (no.469), al-Bukhaaree in *Khalq Af'aalil-'Ibaad* (p.42), at-Tirmidhee (no.2382) who declared it *hasan* and others. Its chain of narration is *saheeh*.

edge in order to be able to narrate it, and does not seek it in order to act upon it." One of the *Salaf* said, "It has reached us that he who seeks *ahaadeeth* merely in order to narrate them will not find the fragrance of Paradise," meaning he whose only intention in seeking them is to be able to narrate them, and not to act upon them.

This is similar to the hatred of the *Salafus-Saalih* (the Pious Predecessors) that a person should put himself forward to give religious verdicts (*fataawa*) and to crave them, and to hasten to it, and to do it to excess. Ibn Lahee'ah reports from 'Ubaydullaah ibn Abee Ja'far in *mursal* form from the Prophet (ﷺ) that he said, *"He who is boldest from you in giving religious verdicts, will be the boldest in proceeding to the Fire."*[33] 'Alqamah said, "They used to say, 'The boldest of you in giving religious verdicts is the one having the least knowledge.'"

Al-Baraa' said, "I met a hundred and twenty of the Ansaar from the Companions of Allaah's Messenger (ﷺ) and when one of them was asked about a matter there was not a single man amongst them except that he wished that his brother would suffice him (by answering)."[34] In a narration there occurs the addition, "...so this one would refer it to another, and he would refer it to someone else until it would eventually return to the first one." From Ibn Mas'ood, *radiyallaahu*

---

[33] It is reported by ad-Daarimee (1/57) and its chain of narration is weak since it is *mursal* (i.e. there is a missing link or links between the last narrator and the Prophet (ﷺ)).

[34] This saying is reported by ad-Daarimee (1/53) and Ibn 'Abdul-Barr in *al-Jaami'* (2/163). However it is the saying of 'Abdur-Rahmaan ibn Abee Laylaa and not the saying of al-Baraa', and its chain of narration is *saheeh*. As for the saying of al-Baraa', then it is, "I saw three hundred of the people of Badr, there was not a single one of them except that he loved that someone else should take his place in answering." It is reported by Ibnul-Mubaarak in *az-Zuhd* (no.58), Ibn Sa'd (6/11) and others and its *isnaad* contains Aboo Ishaaq as-Sabee'ee who is acceptable (*sadooq*) except that he was a *mudallis* and reports it without stating that he heard it directly.

'anhu, who said, "The one who gives a religious verdict to the people about everything that he is asked is indeed insane."[35]

'Umar ibn 'Abdul-'Azeez was asked about a question and replied, "I am not one who is bold about giving religious verdicts." He also wrote to one of his governors, "By Allaah I am not one who craves after giving religious verdicts, as long as I can find a way to avoid it."

Ibn Yameenah said, "This affair is not for those who love that the people should have need of them, rather this affair is only for those who love that someone can be found to take their place." It is also reported from him that he said, "The most knowledgeable of people concerning religious verdicts is the one who is most often silent, and the most ignorant of people about them is the one who speaks the most with regard to them."[36]

Sufyaan ath-Thawree said, "We reached the scholars and they used to hate answering questions and giving religious verdicts until they could find no way out except to give a verdict, but if they were relieved of having to do so then that was more beloved to them."

Imaam Ahmad said, "He who puts himself forward to give religious verdicts has put himself forward to something very serious, unless he is forced into it through necessity." It was said to him, "Then which is better: for him to speak or to remain silent?" He said, "It is more beloved to us that he should withhold." It was said, "But if there is a

---

[35] Reported by Ibn 'Abdul-Barr (2/164-165), al-Khateeb in *al-Faqeeh wal-Mutafaqqih* (2/197-198) and Aboo Khaithamah in *al-'Ilm* (no.10) and its chain of narration is *saheeh*.

[36] Reported by al-Khateeb in *al-Faqeeh wal-Mutafaqqih* (2/166) and its *isnaad* is weak.

necessity?" So he started saying, "Necessity! Necessity!" And he said, "It is safer for him to withhold."

So those who give religious verdicts should realise that they are transmitting Allaah's orders and prohibitions and that he will be made to stand to account and be questioned about it. Ar-Rabee' ibn Khaitham said, "O givers of religious verdicts! Look and see how you are giving verdicts." 'Amr ibn Deenaar said to Qataadah when he sat to give religious verdicts, "Do you realise the affair that you have fallen into? You have come between Allaah and His worshippers and say, 'This is correct and this is not correct.'"[37] From Ibnul-Munkadir who said, "The scholar enters between Allaah and His creation, so let him look and see how he enters between them."[38]

When Ibn Seereen was asked about anything pertaining to the permissible and the forbidden his colour would change and he would alter so that he would not seem to be the same person.[39] When an-Nakhaa'ee was asked something then hatred would be seen upon his face and he would say, "Could you not find someone else to ask other than me?" He also said, "I spoke and if I had found any way out I would not have spoken, and indeed a time when I am the scholar of Koofah is an evil time."[40]

---

[37] Reported by al-Khateeb in *al-Faqeeh wal-Mutafaqqih* (2/168).

[38] Reported with variations in wording by ad-Daarimee (1/53) and al-Khateeb in *al-Faqeeh wal-Mutafaqqih* (2/168) and its *isnaad* is *saheeh.*

[39] Reported by Ibn Sa'd (7/195), al-Khateeb in *al-Faqeeh wal-Mutafaqqih* (2/167) and its *isnaad* is *saheeh.*

[40] Reported in meaning by Aboo Khaithamah in *al-'Ilm* (no.131).

It is related that Ibn 'Umar, *radiyallaahu 'anhumaa*, said, "You ask us for religious verdicts in such a manner that it is as if we are people who are not going to be questioned about the verdicts that we give you."[41] Also from Muhammad ibn Waasi' who said, "The first of those who will be called to account are the scholars." It is reported about Maalik, *radiyallaahu 'anhu*, that when he was asked about a matter it was as if he were standing between Paradise and the Hell-Fire.[42]

One of the scholars also said to a person who used to give religious verdicts, "When you are asked about a matter then do not let your concern be to release and find a way out for the questioner, but rather to release and save your own self."[43] Another said, "If you are asked about a matter then consider - if you find a way out of it then speak, otherwise remain silent." The sayings of the *Salaf* about this are too many to quote and gather.

Also relating to this is the hatred of entering upon and coming near to the sovereigns, this is the means used by the worldly scholars to attain worldly status and position. Imaam Ahmad, Aboo Daawood, at-Tirmidhee and an-Nasaa'ee report from the *hadeeth* of Ibn 'Abbaas, *radiyallaahu 'anhumaa*, from the Prophet (ﷺ) who said, *"He who settles in the desert becomes coarse/hardhearted, and he who pur-*

---

[41] Reported by al-Fasawee (1/490) and al-Khateeb in *al-Faqeeh wal-Mutafaqqih* (2/168) and its *isnaad* is weak.

[42] Reported by al-Khateeb in *al-Faqeeh wal-Mutafaqqih* (2/167) and its *isnaad* is weak.

[43] The one who said this was 'Umar ibn Khaldah az-Zurqee and he was speaking to Rabee'ah ibn Abee 'Abdir-Rahmaan. This narration is reported with very close wordings by al-Fasawee (1/556-557), Aboo Nu'aym in *al-Hilyah* (3/260-261) and al-Khateeb in *al-Faqeeh wal-Mutafaqqih* (2/169) and its *isnaad* is *saheeh*.

sues the game will become negligent, and he who visits the kings will be put to trial."[44]

Ahmad and Aboo Daawood report its like from the *hadeeth* of Aboo Hurairah, *radiyallaahu 'anhu*, from the Prophet (ﷺ) and there occurs in this *hadeeth*, *"...And no one increases in nearness to the king except that he becomes further away from Allaah."*[45]

Ibn Maajah also reports from the *hadeeth* of Ibn 'Abbaas, *radiyallaahu 'anhumaa*, from the Prophet (ﷺ) who said, *"Indeed some people from my Ummah will boast religious knowledge and will recite the Qur'aan and will say, 'We will enter upon the rulers and attain a share of their worldly riches, but will remain separate from them with our religion. But that will not be the case just as nothing will be harvested from the tragacanth (al-Qataad)*[46]*except thorns. Likewise nothing will be gained from nearness to them except sins."*[47]

---

[44] Reported by Ahmad (1/357), Aboo Daawood (transl. 2/803/no.2853), at-Tirmidhee (no.2256) who declared it *saheeh*, an-Nasaa'ee (7/195-196) and others. Its *isnaad* is weak since it contains Aboo Moosa an unknown narrator. However it has another chain of narration with al-Baihaqee in *Shu'abul-Eemaan* (3/2/248) which strengthens and supports it if Allaah wills.

[45] Reported by Ahmad (2/371,440), Aboo Daawood (transl. 2/803/2854) and al-Baihaqee in *Shu'abul-Eemaan* (3/2/248) and its *isnaad* contains al-Hasan ibn al-Hakam an-Nakhaa'ee who is generally acceptable but makes mistakes. I say: The first *isnaad* strengthens it, and Allaah knows best.

[**Translator's note**: This second narration is declared weak by Shaikh al-Albaanee in *Da'eef Sunan Abee Daawood*.]

[46] A thorny bush which grows in Arabia (of the genus Astagalus). [translators note]

[47] Reported by Ibn Maajah (no.255 and its *isnaad* contains al-Waleed ibn Muslim who is a *mudallis* reporting with *'an'anah*, and also 'Ubaydullaah ibn Abee Burdah who is acceptable only when supported in his narration - otherwise he is weak.

It is also reported by at-Tabaraanee and his wording is, *"Indeed some people from my Ummah will recite the Qur'aan and delve into the Religion. Shaitaan will come to them and say, 'If only you would enter upon the rulers and benefit from their worldly riches and remain separate from them with your Religion.' Indeed that will not be the case, just as nothing will be harvested from the tragacanth except thorns. Likewise nothing will be gained from nearness to them except sins."* Also at-Tirmidhee reports from the *hadeeth* of Aboo Hurairah, *radiyallaahu 'anhu,* from the Prophet (ﷺ) that he said, *"Seek Allaah's refuge from the pit of grief." They said: 'And what is the pit of grief? 'He said: "A valley in Hell from which Hell (itself) seeks refuge a hundred times a day." It was said: "who will enter it O Messenger of Allaah?" He said: "Those reciters who do their actions for show."*[48] Ibn Maajah reports its like and adds: *"...And from the most hated of reciters to Allaah are those who visit the tyrant rulers."*[49] Its like is also reported from the *hadeeth* of 'Alee, *radiyallaahu 'anhu,* from the Prophet (ﷺ).

One of the greatest things that is to be feared for one who enters upon the oppressive rulers is that he will agree with their falsehood and help them to commit oppression even if it is only by remaining silent and failing to forbid them. So if he enters upon them seeking and aspiring to status and authority, then he will not forbid them, rather he is liable to declare some of their evil actions to be good in order that he may be raised in their eyes so that they help him to attain his goal.

---

[48] Reported by at-Tirmidhee (no. 2383) and its *isnaad* is very weak, containing one narrator who is weak (*da'eef*) and another who is abandoned (*matrook*).

[49] Reported by Ibn Maajah (no.256) with the same *isnaad* as the previous one and it is also reported by at-Tabaraanee in *al-Awsat* with close wording as occurs in *Majma' uz-Zawaa'id* (7/168) and al-Haithumee said: It contains Bukayr ibn Shihaab ad-Daa'ifaanee who is weak.

Imaam Ahmad, at-Tirmidhee, an-Nasaa'ee and Ibn Hibbaan in his *Saheeh* report from the *hadeeth* of Ka'b ibn 'Ujrah, *radiyallaahu 'anhu*, from the Prophet (ﷺ) who said, *"There will be after me rulers, so he who enters upon them and agrees with them in their falsehood and helps them in their wrongdoing - then he has no connection with me and I have no connection with him, and he will not come to me at the Pond (Hawd). However he who does not enter upon them, and does not help them in their wrongdoing, and does not agree with them in their falsehood - then he is from me and I am from him, and he will come to me at the Pond-Lake (Hawd)."*[50]

Imaam Ahmad reports the meaning of this *hadeeth* from the *hadeeth* of Hudhayfah, *radiyallaahu 'anhu*, and Ibn 'Umar, *radiyallaahu 'anhumaa*, and Khabbaab ibn al-Aratt, and Aboo Sa'eed al-Khudree and an-Nu'maan ibn Basheer, *radiyallaahu 'anhum·*

Also many of the *Salaf* used to forbid entering upon the rulers even for those who wanted to enjoin the good and forbid the evil. From those who forbade this were 'Umar ibn 'Abdul-'Azeez, Ibnul-Mubaarak, ath-Thawree and other scholars. Ibnul-Mubaarak said, "In our view the one who orders and forbids them is not the one who enters upon them and orders and forbids them. Rather the one who orders and forbids them is the one who keeps away from them." The reason for this is the corruption that it is to be feared may be caused through entering upon them. This is because a person may deceive himself whilst he is at a distance from them into thinking that he will order and forbid them and behave firmly with them. However when he sees them face to face his soul inclines towards them since love of status is concealed in his soul - therefore he flatters them and is lenient with them. He may even be charmed by them and come to love them particularly if they treat him kindly and bestow favours upon

---

[50] Reported by Ahmad (4/243), at-Tirmidhee (no.2259), an-Nasaa'ee (17/160, 160-161) and others and its *isnaad* is *saheeh*.

him and he accepts that from them. Something similar to this occurred with 'Abdullaah ibn Taawoos along with one of the rulers in the presence of his father - so Taawoos rebuked him for that.

Also Sufyaan ath-Thawree wrote to 'Abbaad ibn 'Abbaad and said, "...Beware of the rulers and of approaching and mixing with them in any of the affairs. Beware of being deluded so that it is said that you should do so in order to intercede with them for someone, or to help the oppressed or stop oppression. This is a deception of Iblees, and is taken by the wicked reciters as a means of advancing themselves. When you have occasion to receive questions and of having to give religious rulings then avail yourself of that and do not compete with them in it. Also beware of being one of those who loves that his saying should be acted upon, publicised and listened to - so that when it is abandoned the effect it has upon him is noticed. Beware of leadership since love of leadership may be more beloved to a person than that of gold and silver. It is something whose reality is obscure and hidden and not comprehended except by the wise and perceptive scholars. So take care of your own soul and act with correct intention, and know that a matter is approaching the people which is such that a man will desire death due to it. *Was-Salaam.*"[51]

Also pertaining to this is the hatred of a man's making himself known as being a person of knowledge, abstemiousness and Religion, or his manifesting actions, sayings and miraculous blessings in order that people should visit him, seek blessings through him, request supplication from him and kiss his hand - and he loves that, habituates it, is made happy by it, and seeks after it.

In this regard the Pious Predecessors (*as-Salafus-Saaliheen*) used to have utmost hate of fame. From those noted for this were Ayyoob, an-Nakhaa'ee, Sufyaan, Ahmad and other wise scholars. The same

---

[51] It is quoted by Aboo Nu'aym in *al-Hilyah* (6/376-377).

was the case with al-Fudayl and Daawood at-Taa'ee and others who avoided the allurement of this world and were people of insight. They used to criticise themselves severely and take great pains to hide their actions. It happened that a man entered upon Daawood at-Taa'ee and he asked him why he had come. So he replied, "I came to visit you." So he said, "Then you have reached a great deal of good in that you have visited someone for Allaah's sake, however I can only look to what I will face tomorrow when it will be said to me, 'Who are you that you deserve to be visited? Are you one of those who remain aloof from worldly allurements?' No, by Allaah. 'Are you one of the (great) worshippers?' No, by Allaah. 'Are you one of the righteous servants?' No, by Allaah... and he mentioned a number of the good qualities in this manner, then he began rebuking himself and saying, 'O Daawood! When you were a youth you were wicked, and when you have grown old you have become a person who does actions for show - and this is worse than being a sinner."

Muhammad ibn Waasi' used to say, "If sins had an odour then nobody would be able to sit with me." When anyone used to enter upon Ibraaheem an-Nakhaa'ee and he was reciting from the *mushaf* he would cover it up. Uways and others who avoided the worldly allurements would, if they became known in a place, move on from it.

Many of the *Salaf* would also hate that anyone should ask them to make supplication for them, and they would say to those who requested it, "Who am I?" Amongst those whom that is reported from are 'Umar ibn al-Khattaab and Hudhayfah ibn al-Yamaan, *radiyallaahu 'anhumaa*, and likewise Maalik ibn Deenaar. An-Nakhaa'ee also used to hate that anyone should request him to supplicate for them. A man wrote to Ahmad asking for him to supplicate for him, so Ahmad said, "If we are to supplicate for this, then who will supplicate for us?"

Once the exertions of a pious man in worship were described to a ruler and so he decided to visit him. When the man heard of this, he sat at the side of the road eating a great deal and he paid no attention to the ruler. So the ruler said, "There is no good in this one," and he went back. So the man said, "All praises and thanks are for Allaah who sent him back whilst he was finding fault with me."

This matter is very vast, and there is a fine point here. It is that a person may criticise himself before some people, intending thereby that the people should see that he is modest and therefore be raised in their eyes and be praised by them. This is one of the subtle doors of ostentation/show (*riyaa'*) and the Pious Predecessors have warned us about it. Mutarrif ibn 'Abdullaah ibn ash-Shikhkheer said, "It is sufficient to amount to conceit that a person criticises himself in a gathering intending only self-adornment, and this to Allaah is foolishness."

This World and the Hereafter

From what we have mentioned it will be clear that love of wealth and leadership and craving after them destroys a person's Religion (*Deen*) to the point that nothing except what Allaah wills remains of it, just as the Prophet (ﷺ) informed.

The root of love of wealth and status is love of this world, and the root of love of this world is following of desires. Wahb ibn Munabbih said, "From following desires comes desire for this world, and from desire for this world comes love of wealth and status, and from love of wealth and status comes making lawful that which is forbidden." This is a fine saying, since love of wealth and status is caused by desire for this world, and desire for this world is brought about by following one's desires. This is because one's desires call to desire for this world and love of wealth and status in it. But *taqwaa* prevents one from following desires and prevents love of this world. Allaah, the Most High, said:

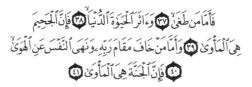

"Then, for such as had transgressed all bounds, and had preferred the life of this world, their abode will be Hell-Fire; but as for him who feared standing before his Lord, and restrained himself from impure evil desires, and lusts - verily, Paradise will be his abode."

an-Naazi'aat (79):37-41

Allaah, the Most High, has also described the people of the Fire as being people who formerly possessed wealth and authority in a number of places in His Book. He, the Most High, says:

"But as for him who will be given his record in his left hand, will say: 'I wish that I had not been given my record! and that I had not known how my account is? I wish, would that it had been my end (death)! My wealth has not availed me, my authority and argument (to defend myself) have gone from me.'"

al-Haaqqah (69):25-29

Know that that soul loves to attain rank and position above its like and this is what produces pride and envy. However the intelligent one strives for everlasting and perpetual rank which is in Allaah's pleasure, and in nearness to Him, and he turns away from fleeting and short-lived rank which is followed by Allaah's Wrath and Anger and means the person's downfall, lowness and his distance from Allaah and being banished away from Him. So this is the second kind of eminence which is blameworthy and it is wrongful haughtiness and eminence upon the earth. As for the first type of eminence and wishing for it - then that is praiseworthy, Allaah, the Most High, says,

"And for this let (all) those strive who want to strive."

al-Mutaffifeen (83):26

Al-Hasan [al-Basree] said, "If you see a man competing with you with regard to this world then compete with him concerning the Hereafter."

Wuhayb ibn al-Ward said, "If you are able to make sure that no one precedes you in hastening towards Allaah then do so."

Muhammad ibn Yoosuf al-Asbahaanee, the worshipper, said, "If a person hears of another person or knows of another person who is more obedient to Allaah than him, then that should grieve him."

Someone else said, "If a man hears or knows of another man who is more obedient to Allaah than himself and this causes his heart to break - then this is not a case of vanity."

A man said to Maalik ibn Deenaar, "I saw in a dream a caller calling out, 'O People! The time for departing and the time for moving on has come.' But I did not see anyone departing except Muhammad ibn Waasi'. So Maalik cried out and fainted.

So it is correct to vie for the levels of rank in the Hereafter and to seek and aspire to that by hastening in that which leads to it, and that a person should not be satisfied with aspiring for a lower rank when it is within his power to aspire for that which is higher.

But as for the second eminence which is cut off and followed by regret, grief, humiliation, shame and inferiority - then it is prescribed to avoid this and to turn away from it for many reasons. From these is that a servant should look to the evil results in the Hereafter of seeking status in this world through authority and leadership - for those who do not discharge its duties justly. Also from them is that the servant should consider the punishment awaiting the unjust and the proud and haughty and those who seek to compete with Allaah's cloak of Pride.

It is reported in the *Sunan* that the Prophet (ﷺ) said, "*The haughty will be raised up on the Day of Resurrection like tiny ants in the shape of men, humiliation will cover them from every side. They will be led in to a place of confinement in Hell-Fire called Boolas. They will be covered by the Fire of Fires. They will be given to drink the festering pus flowing from the inhabitants of the Fire.*"[52] In a different narration reported elsewhere there occurs in this *hadeeth*, "*The people will tread upon them with their feet.*"[53] In a further narration reported through a different chain there occurs, "*Jinn, humans and animals will tread upon them with their feet until Allaah carries out judgement between His servants.*"

A man asked permission of 'Umar, *radiyallaahu 'anhu*, to address the people, so he said to him, 'I fear that if you address the people you will feel that you are better than them and so Allaah will place you beneath their feet on the Day of Resurrection.'

Also from the reasons[54] for this is that the servant should consider the reward in store for those who are humble for Allaah's sake in this world, and that they will attain eminence in the Hereafter since whoever humbles himself for Allaah then Allaah will raise him in rank. Also from the reasons for this, and it is not something in the control of the servant, rather it is from the Bounty and Mercy of Allaah and it is that those servants of His who know Him and who abstain for His sake from temporary wealth and status - in exchange for that in this world Allaah gives them the honour of *taqwaa* and the respect of the creation. They will also taste the sweetness of having knowledge of

---

[52] Reported by Ahmad (2/179), al-Bukhaaree in *al-Aadaabul-Mufrad* (no.557) and at-Tirmidhee (no.2492) who declared it *hasan* and its *isnaad* is *hasan*.

[53] Reported by 'Abdullaah ibn Ahmad in his additions to *az-Zuhd* (p.22) and its *isnaad* contains 'Ataa' ibn Muslim al-Khaffaaf who is generally acceptable except that he makes many mistakes as occurs in *at-Taqreeb* of Ibn Hajr, and Ahmad disapproved of this narration as occurs in *Taareekh Baghdaad* (12/294).

[54] i.e. the reasons which should cause a person to avoid seeking after eminence in this world.

Him, and of *Eemaan* and obedience - and this is the good and pleasant life promised to those men and women who act righteously and are Believers. This good and pleasant life is not tasted by the kings of this world, nor by those who aspire to authority and status. Ibraaheem ibn Adham, *rahimahullaah*, said, "If the kings and their sons knew that which we delight in, they would contend with us for it by the use of the sword."

So whoever is granted that by Allaah, is preoccupied by it from seeking fleeting status and temporary eminence, Allaah, the Most High, says:

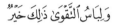

"The rainment of righteousness - that is the best."

al-A'raaf (7):26

He, the Most High, says:

مَن كَانَ يُرِيدُ ٱلْعِزَّةَ فَلِلَّهِ ٱلْعِزَّةُ جَمِيعًا

"Whoever desires honour, power and glory then to Allaah belong all honour, power and glory."

Faatir (35):10

There occurs in some narrations that Allaah, the Mighty and Majestic, says, *"I am the Mighty and whoever wishes for honour then let him be obedient to the Mighty, and whoever wishes for honour in this world and the Hereafter - then let him have taqwaa."*

Hajjaaj ibn Artaat used to say, "Love of status has killed me." So Sawwaar said, "If you had *taqwaa* of Allaah then you would attain status."

Concerning this there is the poem:
"Indeed *taqwaa* is honour and nobility
    Whereas your love of this world is humiliation and a sickness
And a servant having *taqwaa* will not suffer loss
    If he truly has *taqwaa*...*"

Saalih al-Baajee said, "Obedience is authority and the one who obeys Allaah is one in authority given authority over the rulers. Do you not see the awe they hold for him in their hearts. If he speaks they accept it and if he commands they obey." Then he said, "It is fitting that one who serves You well and then You bestow favour upon him - that through Your love the tyrants are humble before him and have awe of him due to the position he holds in their hearts, which is due to the awe that he has for You in his heart, and every good that is from You if with Your chosen servants."

One of the *Salafus-Saaliheen* said, "Who can be more fortunate than one who is obedient (to Allaah) since all good lies in obedience (to Him)? Indeed the one obedient to Allaah is a sovereign in this world and the Hereafter."

Dhun-Noon said, "Who is more noble and honourable than one who is cut off from everyone except the One who has sovereignty of everything in His Hand?"

Muhammad ibn Sulaymaan - the governor of Basrah, entered upon Hammaad ibn Salamah and sat before him asking him questions, and he said, "O Aboo Salamah! How is it that every time I look at you I tremble due to fear of you?" He said, "Since if the scholar intends by his knowledge the Face of Allaah everything fears him, but if he wishes by it to increase in treasures then he himself fears everything."

Likewise someone said, "In accordance with your fear of Allaah the creation will fear you, and in accordance with your love of Him the creation will love you, and in accordance with your preoccupation with Allaah the creation will be occupied in carrying out that which you are preoccupied from."

It happened one day that 'Umar ibn al-Khattaab, *radiyallaahu 'anhu*, was walking and behind him were some of the older *muhaajirs*, so he turned round to them and saw that they fell upon their knees out of awe of him. So 'Umar, *radiyallaahu 'anhu*, wept and said, "O Allaah You know that I have more fear of You than them, so forgive me."

Al-'Umaree the *zaahid* (one who avoids the allurements of this world) once went out to Koofah towards ar-Rasheed in order to admonish and forbid him, and fear spread through ar-Rasheed's army when they heard of his arrival such that if an enemy army of a hundred thousand had approached it would not have caused them greater fear.

It was also the case that no one was able to question al-Hasan due to their awe of him, and his closest students would gather together and ask each other to ask him questions. But then when they attended his gathering they could not bring themselves to ask him - to the point that it would sometimes continue for a year, due to their awe of him. Likewise the people used to fear to ask Anas ibn Maalik questions and about this someone said,
"The answer is left and not mentioned again due to awe,
       And the questioners sit with their chins lowered -
The light of dignity and honour, the sovereign of *taqwaa*.
       So he is the one who inspires awe and he is not a sovereign."

Badeel al-'Uqailee used to say, "Whoever intends by his knowledge the Face of Allaah, the Most High, then Allaah turns with His Face to him, and turns the hearts of the servants to him, and whoever acts for other than Allaah, then Allaah turns His Face away from him and turns the hearts of the servants away from him."

Muhammad ibn Waasi' said, "If a servant turns to Allaah with his heart then Allaah turns to him with the hearts of the Believers."

Aboo Yazeed al-Bustaamee, *rahimahullaah*, said, "I have divorced this world finally and irrevocably three times and have turned to my Lord alone, and called upon Him for help, 'O my Lord I supplicate to You with the supplication of one who has nobody left but You.' He knew the truth of my supplication from my heart and my despairing of myself, then the first part of the answer to this supplication was that He caused me to forget my own self totally and He placed the creation in front of me despite my turning away from them." He used to be visited from the various lands, and when he saw the people crowding to him he said,
"Woe to me I have become something -
    Without preparing for that at all -
I have become a master to them all - because I am a slave to You.
    And in the heart are matters - which cannot be counted.
However concealing my condition - is more fitting for me and more correct."

Wahb ibn Munabbih wrote to Makhool, "To proceed. By what is apparent from your knowledge you have attained status and position with the people. By what is hidden from your knowledge seek position with Allaah and nearness to Him, and know that one of the two positions prevents from the other."

The meaning of this is that the apparent knowledge - i.e. learning the duties, laws, rulings, religious verdicts, narrations and admonitions and so on - which is apparent to the people will cause a person to gain status and position with them. But the hidden knowledge which is stored in the heart - i.e. knowledge of Allaah, fear and love of Him, being wary of Him, being satisfied with Him, and longing to meet Him, placing reliance upon Him, being pleased with what he has decreed, turning away from worldly matters which will pass away and turning to the Hereafter which will remain. All of this causes a person to have position and nearness to Allaah. Each of these two positions prevents the other. So he who remains and stops at the position of worldly status he gains with the people and preoccupies himself with what he has attained with them due to his apparent knowledge. So his only concern is to preserve this station with the people and to remain in it and to cultivate it, and having fear that it will pass away. Then this will be all that he receives from Allaah the Most High, and he is therefore cut off from him. So he is just like the one about whom someone said, "Woe to the one who receives this world as his portion from Allaah."

As-Sariyy as-Saqatee used to be pleased by what he saw of the knowledge of al-Junayd, and his fine speech and speed in answering, so he said to him one day after having asked him a question and receiving a good answer, "I fear that your share of the world has been given to you in your tongue." So al-Junayd used to weep thereafter because of that.

But he who occupies himself with improving his position with Allaah, the Most High, through what we have mentioned of hidden knowledge, then he will reach Allaah - and he will be preoccupied with Him from all else. This will prevent him from seeking for position amongst the people, yet despite this Allaah will indeed give him position and status in the hearts of the people - even if he does not want that, does not settle for it and flees from it and runs away from it for fear that the creation will cut him off from Allaah, the Majestic. Allaah, the Most High, says,

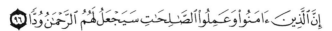

"Verily, those who believe and work deeds of righteousness, the Most Beneficient (Allaah) will bestow love for them."

Maryam (19):96

Meaning Allaah will put love for them in the hearts of His servants.

There also occurs in the *hadeeth, "When Allaah loves a servant He calls out, 'O Jibreel! Indeed I love so and so, so love him.' So Jibreel loves him [so Jibreel calls out to the inhabitants of the heavens, 'Allaah loves so and so, so love him]' so the inhabitants of the heavens love him and then he is granted acceptance upon the earth."*[55] The *hadeeth* is well-known and reported in the *Saheeh*.

So in any case seeking after eminence in the Hereafter brings along with it honour in this world, even if the person does not want it and does not seek it. But seeking status in this world will not come together and be combined with honour in the Hereafter. So the fortunate one is he who prefers that which is everlasting to that which passes away, just as occurs in the *hadeeth* of Aboo Moosa, *radiyallaahu 'anhu*, from the Prophet (ﷺ) that he said, *"He who loves this world - then it will harm his Hereafter and he who loves the Hereafter then it will harm his worldly life. So prefer that which will remain to that which will pass away."*[56] It is reported by Imaam Ahmad and others.

---

[55] It is reported with close wordings by Maalik, Ahmad, al-Bukhaaree (transl. 8/41/ no.66).

[56] It is reported by Ahmad (4/412), Ibn Hibbaan (2473: *al-Mawaarid*), al-Haakim (4/308) who declared it *saheeh* and al-Baghawee in *Sharhus-Sunnah* (14/239). Adh-Dhahabee said, "Its chain of narration is disconnected." I say that is between Aboo Moosa and the narrator from him who is al-Muttalib ibn 'Abdullaah.

Abul-Fath al-Bustiyy indeed spoke well when he said:

"Two matters will be separate, you will not see them both -

Desiring one anothers company and meeting together,

Seeking the good of the Hereafter along with leadership and eminence -

So abandon that which will pass away in favour of that which will remain."

Here the speech of al-Haafidh Zaynuddeen Ibn Rajab in explanation of the *hadeeth*, *"Two hungry wolves let loose..."* is completed, and all praise and thanks are due to Allaah, and may Allaah send praises and blessings upon our Prophet Muhammad, and his family and true followers, and his Companions, and those who act upon his *Sharee'ah* to the Day of Judgement.

Glossary

Aayah (pl. Aayaat): a Sign of Allaah; a verse of the Qur'aan.

Aayaat: See *Aayah*.

Aboo (Abee, Abaa): father of; used as a means of identification.

'Alaihis-salaam: "may Allaah protect and preserve him." It is said after the name of a Prophet of Allaah or after the name of an angel.

Ahaadeeth: See *Hadeeth*.

'An'anah: a narrator's reporting by saying 'from so and so' not describing exactly in what form it was transmitted to him. This will only affect the authenticity of the narration if the one doing it is a *mudallis*.

Ansaar: "Helpers"; theMuslims of Madeenah who supported the Muslims who migrated from Makkah.

Companions (Ar. *Sahaabah*): the Muslims who saw the Prophet (ﷺ) and died upon Islaam.

Da'eef: weak; unauthentic (narration).

Deen: way of life prescribed by Allaah i.e. Islaam.

Eemaan: faith; to affirm all that was revealed to the Messenger (ﷺ), affirming with the heart, testifying with the tongue and acting with the limbs. The actions of the limbs are from the completeness of *Eemaan*. Faith increases with obedience to Allaah and decreases with disobedience.

Fataawaa: see *fatwa*.

Fatwa (pl. Fataawaa): religious verdict.

Fiqh: the understanding and application of the *Sharee'ah* from its sources.

Hadeeth (pl. **Ahaadeeth**): narration concerning the utterances of the Prophe(ﷺ), his actions or an attribute of his.

Hajj: Pilgrimage to Makkah.

Halaal: permitted under the *Sharee'ah*.

Haraam: prohibited under the *Sharee'ah*.

Hasan: fine; term used for an authentic *hadeeth*, which does not reach the higher category of *Saheeh*.

Ibn: son of; used as a means of identification.

Imaam: leader; leader in *Salaah*, knowledge or *fiqh*; leader of a state.

Isnaad: the chain of narrators linking the collector of the saying to the person quoted.

Jinn: A creation of Allaah created from smokeless fire.

Khaleefah (pl. Khulafaa'): the head of the Islamic government (the *khilaafah*) to whom the oath of allegiance is given.

Khulafaa': see *khaleefah*.

Mudallis: most commonly a narrator who reports things from his Shaikh which he did not directly hear from him but from an intermediate whom he does not name but instead says 'from the Shaikh'. This intermediate may be weak. The scholars of *hadeeth* will only accept the narrations of a *mudallis* when he clearly states that he heard them from the Shaikh, i.e. 'The Shaikh narrated to us...' e.t.c.

Muhaajir: One who migrates from the lands of the disbelievers to the land of the Muslims for the sake of Allaah.

Munqati': (lit. disjoined) An isnaad in which two continuous links are missing in one or more than one place or an unknown narrator is found to join the links.

Mursal: loose; a narration in which a *Successor* narrated directly from the Prophet (ﷺ), i.e. omitting the *Companion* from who he heard it.

Mushaf: The Qur'aan between two covers.

Matrook:(lit. discarded) Where narrators are accused of falsehood in matters other than the narration of the tradition.

Radiyallaahu 'anhu/'anhaa/'anhum/'anhumaa: may Allaah be pleased with him/her/them/both of them.

Rahimahullaah/Rahimahumullaah: may Allaah bestow His mercy upon him/them.

Saheeh: correct; an authentic narration.

Salaf: predecessors; the early Muslims; the Muslims of the first three generations: the *Companions*, the *Successors* and their successors.

Salafus-Saaliheen: pious predecessors; the Muslims of the first three generations: the *Companions*, the *Successors* and their successors.

Shaikh: scholar.

Shaitaan: Satan.

Sharee'ah: the Divine code of Law.

Sunnah: in its broadest sense, the entire *Deen* which the Prophet (ﷺ) came with and taught, i.e. all matters of belief, rulings, manners and actions which were conveyed by the *Companions*. It also includes those matters which the Prophet (ﷺ) established by his sayings, actions and tacit approval - as opposed to *bid'ah* (innovation).

sunnah: an action of the Prophet (ﷺ).

Soorah: a chapter of the Qur'aan.

Taabi'ee (pl. Taabi'een): a Muslim (other than another *Companion*) who met a *Companion*.

Taqwa: *"taqwa* is acting in obedience to Allaah, hoping for His mercy upon light from Him and *Taqwa* is leaving acts of disobedience, out of fear of Him, upon light from Him."

Zaahid: One who practices *zuhd*.

Zuhd: Abstaining from the world and its luxuries.